Therapy HORSES

by Catherine Nichols

Consultant: Sheila Kemper Dietrich
Executive Director, NARHA

PUBLISHING

New York, New York

Credits

Cover and Title Page, © Doug Steley/Alamy; 4, © From Naomi Scott, *Special Needs, Special Horses: A Guide to the Benefits of Therapeutic Riding* (Denton: University of North Texas Press, 2005). Copyright 2005 by Naomi Scott. Reprinted by permission.; 5, © David Handley/ Dorling Kindersley; 6, © From Naomi Scott, Special Needs, *Special Horses: A Guide to the Benefits of Therapeutic Riding* (Denton: University of North Texas Press, 2005). Copyright 2005 by Naomi Scott. Reprinted by permission.; 7, © Jody Miller/MillersReflections; 8, © Gloria McDonald/Wild Mane Photos; 9, © Michael Newman/PhotoEdit Inc.; 10, © Topham Picturepoint/TopFoto/The Image Works; 11, © Topham Picturepoint/TopFoto/The Image Works; 12, © Jacki L. Taylor; 13, © From Naomi Scott, *Special Needs, Special Horses: A Guide to the Benefits of Therapeutic Riding* (Denton: University of North Texas Press, 2005). Copyright 2005 by Naomi Scott. Reprinted by permission.; 14, © Kerry Gross/Bit by Bit Therapeutic Riding Program at Tamarack Stables; 15, © AP Images/Patrick Collard; 16, © Kerry Gross/Bit by Bit Therapeutic Riding Program at Tamarack Stables; 17, © Kerry Gross/Bit by Bit Therapeutic Riding Program at Tamarack Stables; 18, © Tom Ervin/Getty Images/NewsCom.com; 19, © From Naomi Scott, *Special Needs, Special Horses: A Guide to the Benefits of Therapeutic Riding* (Denton: University of North Texas Press, 2005). Copyright 2005 by Naomi Scott. Reprinted by permission.; 20, © Kristin Elliott Leas; 21, © Lance Presnall; 22, © From Naomi Scott, *Special Needs, Special Horses: A Guide to the Benefits of Therapeutic Riding* (Denton: University of North Texas Press, 2005). Copyright 2005 by Naomi Scott. Reprinted by permission; 23, © Michael Newman/ PhotoEdit Inc.; 24, © Carol Lawrence/MCT/Newscom.com; 25, © David Frazier/PhotoEdit Inc.; 26, © Dara MacDonaill/The Irish Times; 27, © Kara Morris; 28, © Adrin Snider/Newport News Daily Press/KRT/Newscom; 29TL, © Kit Houghton/Corbis; 29TR, © Jerry Cooke/Animals Animals Earth Scenes; 29M, © Bob Langrish; 29BL, © Juniors Bildarchiv/Alamy; 29BR, © Robert Maier/Animals Animals Earth Scenes.

Publisher: Kenn Goin
Project Editor: Lisa Wiseman
Creative Director: Spencer Brinker
Photo Researcher: Amy Dunleavy
Design: Stacey May

Library of Congress Cataloging-in-Publication Data

Nichols, Catherine.
  Therapy horses / by Catherine Nichols.
    p. cm. — (Horse power)
  Includes bibliographical references (p.   ) and index.
  ISBN-13: 978-1-59716-400-9 (library binding)
  ISBN-10: 1-59716-400-3 (library binding)
 1. Horsemanship—Therapeutic use—Juvenile literature. 2. Horses—Psychological aspects—
Juvenile literature. 3. Human-animal relationships—Juvenile literature. I. Title.

  RM931.H6N53 2007
  615.8'515—dc22
                                            2006031639

For more information, write to Bearport Publishing Company, Inc., 101 Fifth Avenue, Suite 6R, New York, New York 10003. Printed in the United States of America.

10 9 8 7 6 5 4 3 2 1

Contents

A Four-Legged Friend

It was Brandon's first time on a horse. Although he was nervous, he tried not to show it.

Brandon is not like most other kids his age. He has **cerebral palsy**. Since he can't walk, he usually gets around in a wheelchair. However, Brandon was giving up his wheels for Dancer, his new four-legged friend.

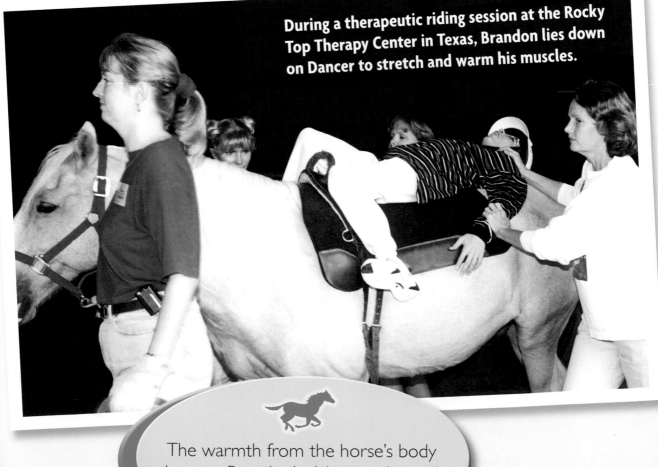

During a therapeutic riding session at the Rocky Top Therapy Center in Texas, Brandon lies down on Dancer to stretch and warm his muscles.

The warmth from the horse's body loosens Brandon's tight muscles and makes him feel better.

After Brandon was placed on top of the horse, he looked down. What a long way to the ground! He took a deep breath. As he had been taught, he gave the **command**. "Walk on!" he said to Dancer. The horse started to move.

Since that first ride, Brandon has had many others. Horseback riding is not just fun for Brandon. It's also **therapeutic**.

Dancer is a palomino just like this horse. These types of horses have golden coats with white manes and tails.

Healing with Horses

Dancer is a therapeutic riding horse. These special animals work with people who have **disabilities**. Riding a horse can help disabled people strengthen their muscles. It also allows them to improve their balance and **coordination**.

Alicia stretches her muscles on her horse, Solomon.

Another **benefit** of riding is that it gives disabled people a sense of freedom and **independence**. If a person is in a wheelchair or uses crutches, riding offers him a chance to get around without help. Many people also end up forming strong bonds with the horses. They often become best friends.

Amy Rynder bonds with her therapeutic riding horse.

Therapeutic riding horses also help increase a person's **self-esteem**.

Riding Centers

Most therapeutic riding horses live and work at special centers. The centers are similar to schools. Disabled people go to them to learn how to ride horses.

At the centers, there are **therapists** who are responsible for each rider's medical care and health. There are also **instructors** who teach riding skills and run classes.

Volunteers who walk next to a horse are called side walkers.

Most places, such as the Rocky Top Therapy Center, also depend on volunteers to keep things running smoothly. They help riders get on and off their horses. They might walk alongside a horse to make sure the rider stays in the right position. Volunteers also take care of the animals. They brush and feed them as well as put on their saddles.

A volunteer helps a disabled rider feed a horse at The Children's Ranch in California.

In the United States, there are more than 750 therapeutic riding centers.

A Rider Who Didn't Give Up

The use of therapeutic riding horses became popular in the 1950s. Liz Hartel, a horseback rider from Denmark, became **paralyzed** after she got **polio**. However, she did not let her disease stop her from riding. When she began to ride her horse, Jubilee, again, she started to regain her strength. In 1952, Liz won a silver medal for riding at the Olympics.

Liz Hartel (right) waits to receive her silver medal at the 1952 Olympics in Helsinki, Finland.

Liz's win **inspired** people. Soon, a program in England was started that helped disabled people ride horses. In no time, therapeutic horseback riding caught on. Today there are riding programs for disabled people all around the world.

Liz and Jubliee

The North American Riding for the Handicapped Association (NARHA) was formed in 1969. This group helps nearly 40,000 people every year.

Special Horses for Special People

Horses come in all shapes and sizes. So it's important to match the horse and rider correctly. Brandon, for instance, was not able to stretch his legs far apart. He needed a small horse with a narrow back. Dancer was a perfect fit!

This boy and his horse are a perfect match.

Therapeutic riding horses can be any **breed**. However, they must be calm. Usually, older horses are calmer than younger ones. For this reason, **mature** animals are preferred. Most horses that do this job are between the ages of 8 and 30.

For some horses, this is a second career. Many animals worked on ranches, in rodeos, or on police forces before working as therapeutic riding horses.

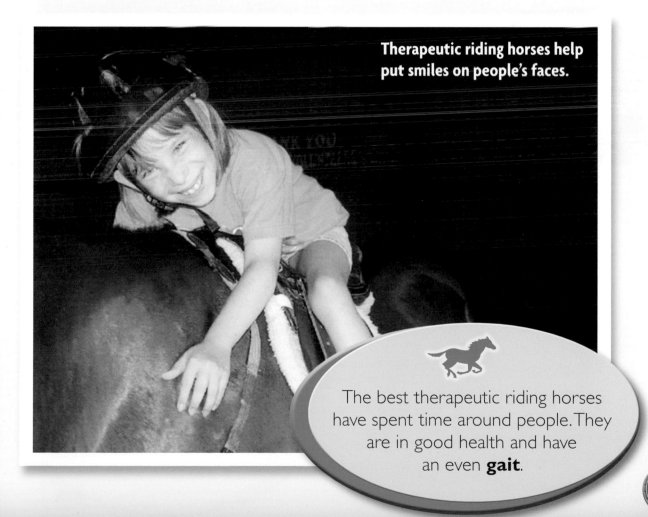

Therapeutic riding horses help put smiles on people's faces.

The best therapeutic riding horses have spent time around people. They are in good health and have an even **gait**.

Being Tested

Before a horse is accepted into a training program, she must be **evaluated**. Instructors need to know if the animal will make a good therapeutic riding horse.

How do they tell? First, instructors test the animal to see if she scares easily. They might bounce a basketball by the horse's legs or throw a stuffed toy near her face. An animal that doesn't flinch or jump will probably be calm enough for the job.

Volunteers at the Bit by Bit Therapeutic Riding program evaluate Isabella to see if she will make a good therapeutic riding horse.

Instructors get special training in how to select therapeutic riding horses.

Many disabled people cannot control their movements. A horse has to get used to this kind of rider. To test the animal, an instructor wiggles and bounces in the saddle to see how the horse reacts.

Therapeutic riding horses must always stay calm around children.

In Training

Once a horse is accepted into a program, the training begins. This process can take several days or up to three months, depending on the horse and the program.

First, the instructors and volunteers introduce the horse to his new home—the ring. He is led around, taught how to stop, to step backward, and to walk around in a circle. The horse also learns how to go over and around poles.

A volunteer instructor lays across this horse during a training session.

During training, horses sniff wheelchairs, bells, rings, and small toys. They need to get used to these items because they may be used in therapeutic riding sessions.

During training, horses are shown ramps and mounting blocks. Riders in wheelchairs use the ramps to get onto their horses. Those who can walk find that standing on a tall block of wood is helpful for getting on the animal.

Volunteers train Isabella to calmly approach the mounting block.

Exercise

Once a horse is trained, she is ready to start working with people. Disabled riders do exercises while on the horse. Some riders sit with one leg on either side of the horse. They practice keeping their balance by holding out their arms. The instructor then leads the horse over logs or around poles.

Therapist Rebecca Reubens and volunteer Kimberly Schuman help Michael keep his balance while on a therapeutic riding horse.

Instructors try to make exercising fun. They might ask a rider to hold his arms out like an airplane, or twist his body like a helicopter.

Other riders are not able to sit up. They lie on their bellies or backs across the horse. The instructor leads the horse around the ring. Volunteers walk on each side to make sure the riders stay safe.

Sometimes riders play games while on horseback. They toss beanbags or throw balls into hoops.

Emma plays basketball while riding her therapeutic riding horse backward. This game helps her stretch her muscles.

Vaulting

Some horses are trained for **vaulting**. In this type of therapy, riders stand, kneel, sit, or lie down while the animal is moving. Vaulting has the same benefits as other forms of therapeutic horseback riding. The only difference is that it is even more fun!

These riders are standing on their horses during a vaulting lesson.

Vaulting is usually done in a group. A class has four to six members. Each person has her own horse and works at her own level. Some riders need a volunteer's help. Others are able to ride on their own.

Vaulting can even be done with two riders on one horse. All riders should wear helmets when vaulting or doing other types of therapeutic horseback riding.

A disabled rider may be in a vaulting class with people who are not disabled.

Making Friends

Some people who have trouble dealing with their **emotions** also work with therapeutic riding horses. A program at the Rocky Top Therapy Center, called Right TRAIL, helps troubled young people. The kids in the program go to the ranch after school. There, they **groom** the horses. Then they take riding and vaulting lessons.

It takes teamwork to saddle a horse.

As young people work together, they learn to trust the horses and one another.

Everyone works in pairs to solve problems. For example, if a horse refuses to have its foot cleaned, the children must figure out how to get the job done. As they succeed in each job, their **confidence** builds. They also learn that every problem has a solution.

A group of kids from The Children's Ranch work together to groom this horse.

Safety First

Therapeutic riding horses work hard to help people. Keeping these animals safe and in good health is important.

After each session, a volunteer walks the horse to cool it down. Next the volunteer takes off the saddle and brushes the animal. If a horse is limping slightly, the volunteer rubs his sore muscles.

A horse massage therapist works on a patient.

Therapists and instructors need to make sure the horses stay healthy. If a horse has a cold, they give him medicine. If he has a cut, they bandage it. For more serious problems, an animal doctor is called to come look at the horse.

A horse can live for 25 years. With good care, some horses can live for 30 years or more.

Showtime

After Brandon had been riding for a few months, he entered the Texas Regional Special Olympics. In this **competition**, riders with disabilities compete against one another in different events. Brandon won a gold medal, a silver medal, and a white ribbon. It is hard to believe that six months earlier he had never been on a horse!

A Special Olympics event held in Ireland

The Special Olympics was started in 1968.

There are other competitions and shows held around the country for disabled people. They give riders like Brandon a chance to show other people what they can do.

Therapeutic riding horses help their riders become stronger and more independent. These animals also provide an important friendship. They deserve their own special medals. They are truly amazing animals.

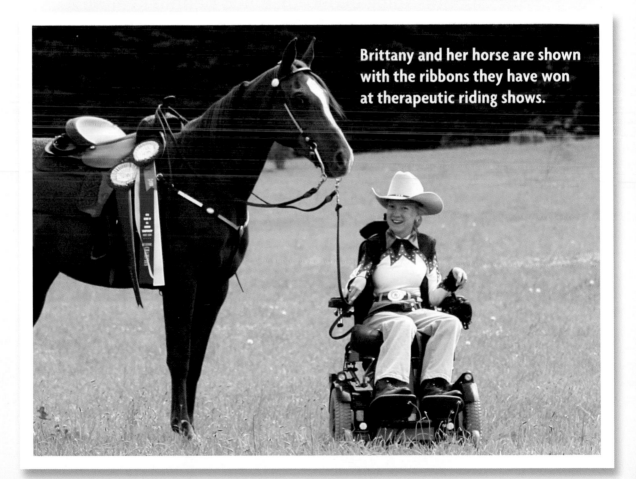

Brittany and her horse are shown with the ribbons they have won at therapeutic riding shows.

Just the Facts

- Disabled riders often don't use a saddle. Instead, they sit on a thick pad so they can feel the warmth of the horse's body.

- Therapeutic riding horses are not the only ones who are trained. Instructors have to go through training to learn how to help disabled riders, too.

- Some programs offer carriage driving. This type of therapeutic riding allows disabled people to sit in a cart behind the horse and steer. The riders benefit by improving their upper body strength and balance.

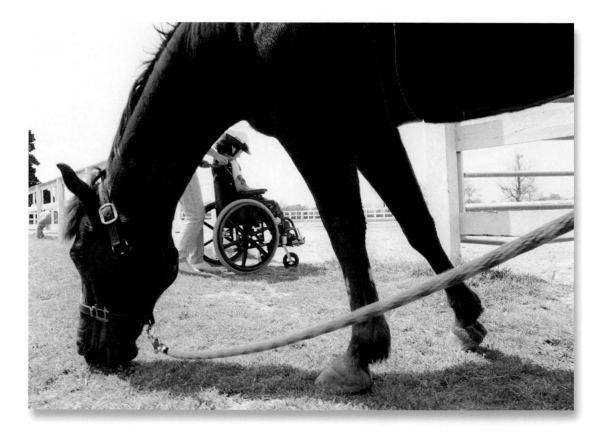

Therapy Horses

Fjord

Morgan Horse

Appaloosa

Paso Fino

Welsh Pony

Glossary

benefit (BEN-uh-fit) something that one is helped by; an advantage

breed (BREED) a type of a certain animal

cerebral palsy (SER-a-bral PAWL-zee) a disability that affects one's control over one's muscles due to brain damage that occurred before, during, or after birth

command (kuh-MAND) an instruction given to be obeyed; an order

competition (*kom*-puh-TISH-uhn) a contest

confidence (KON-fuh-duhnss) having a strong belief in one's abilities

coordination (koh-*or*-duh-NAY-shun) control over one's movements

disabilities (*diss*-uh-BIL-uh-teez) conditions that make it hard for people to go about their daily activities

emotions (i-MOH-shuhnz) strong feelings such as sadness or anger

evaluated (i-VAL-yoo-*ayt*-id) judged how good something is

gait (GATE) the way a horse lifts its feet while walking

groom (GROOM) to brush and comb a horse's coat

independence (*in*-di-PEN-duhnss) being able to do things on one's own; freedom

inspired (in-SPYE-urd) encouraged others to do things

instructors (in-STRUHKT-urz) people who teach

mature (muh-CHUR) older; behaving in a sensible way

paralyzed (PA-ruh-lyezd) unable to move parts of one's body

polio (POH-lee-oh) a disease that attacks the brain and spinal cord and can sometimes lead to paralysis

self-esteem (SELF-ess-TEEM) feeling full of pride or respect for oneself

therapeutic (ther-uh-PYOO-tic) having to do with treatment to improve an illness or heal an injury

therapists (THER-uh-pists) people who are professionally trained and licensed to help others improve or strengthen their level of function

vaulting (VAWLT-ing) a type of therapy in which gymnastic exercises are performed on a moving horse

Bibliography

Scott, Naomi. *Special Needs, Special Horses: A Guide to the Benefits of Therapeutic Riding*. Denton, Texas: University of North Texas Press (2005).

archives.seattletimes.nwsource.com/cgi-bin/texis.cgi/web/vortex/display?slug=healthhorsetherapy14&date=20040714&query=javaica

www.equisearch.com/horses_riding_training/sports/therapeutic/eqhistory1654

www.pbs.org/wnet/nature/horses/freedom.html

Read More

Budd, Jackie. *Horses*. New York: Kingfisher (1995).

Hansen, Rosanna. *Caring Animal*. New York: Children's Press (2003).

Oliver, Clare. *Animals Helping with Special Needs (Animals That Help Us)*. New York: Franklin Watts (2000).

Presnall, Judith Janda. *Animals on the Job: Horse Therapists*. San Diego, CA: KidHaven Press (2001).

Learn More Online

To learn more about therapeutic riding horses, visit **www.bearportpublishing.com/HorsePower**

Index

About the Author

Catherine Nichols has written many books for children, including several on animals. As a teenager, she worked as a volunteer in a horse stable and rode horses. She lives in Beacon, New York.